Health Home and Happiness

What Can I Eat Now?

30 Days on the Gut and Psychology Syndrome (GAPS) Introduction Diet

Introduction

What Can I Eat Now?

30 Days on the GAPS ™ Introduction Diet~ Meal Plans and Tips.

Cara Comini

A 30 day collection of recipes for the introduction portion of the diet; 5 days on each of the 6 stages.

Appetites vary. Recipes are designed for a family of 3-4, but how much your own family eats can greatly vary.

Remember, if you get stuck on any stage, you can go back and repeat any of the recipes in the previous days for variety.

This meal plan is a guide for those who anticipate being able to go through the introduction portion of the GAPS diet quickly. If you have many digestive issues, you may need to spend more time on each stage than I give here. Your individual needs will vary, this is just a guide to help with meal planning.

GAPS™ and Gut and Psychology Syndrome™ are the trademark and copyright of Dr. Natasha Campbell-McBride. The right of Dr. Natasha Campbell-McBride to be identified as the author of this work has been asserted by her in accordance with the Copyright, Patent and Designs Act 1988.

Before You Start

The GAPS Diet is a wonderfully healing diet, but it does take preparation both physically in the way of making sure your kitchen is set up to cook the foods allowed on the GAPS Intro, and mentally as it means saying 'no' to foods that are causing trouble right now so that you can say 'yes' to health as you progress on the diet.

2 Weeks Before

Order Gut and Psychology Syndrome book and begin reading. The following recommendations are based on the January 2011 edition. It is recommended to read the entire book, but since not everyone will (oh yes, I'm a mom too, I understand), here are the bare minimums to gain understanding of the foundations of the GAPS diet, see how Dr. Natasha herself explains the Introduction Diet, and then specific reading that you will note below to fit your needs.

Required Reading:

- Chapters 1-7; pages 9-65
- Introduction Diet: pages 142-152
- Any specific condition you are dealing with- look in the index for things like eczema, ADD, epilepsy, constipation, diarrhea, etc. and read associated pages. You can note pages here

- _____
- _____
- _____
- _____
- _____
- _____

Next: Source organic vegetables, grassfed meats, pastured eggs, butter, and possibly milk - During the introduction diet we eat lots of vegetables and meat; eggs, butter, and milk are added in small quantities if tolerated. If you do not already know where to find the following vegetables, look at your local health food store, farmer's markets, meet some local farmers, and talk to your local Weston A Price chapter if necessary. Compare prices and quality so you know where to shop during intro.

- Cabbage
- Carrots
- Broccoli
- Onions
- Winter squash such as butternut
- Summer squash such as zucchini
- Cauliflower

- Beef
- Lamb
- Wild caught whole fish (such as trout)
- Game meat (optional)
- Eggs

Consider what supplements you will stop taking

It is essential to avoid 'GAPS illegal' ingredients to get the benefits of the diet, especially the more restrictive Introduction diet! We don't want all our hard work to be compromised by a simple supplement.

Medications:

Before discontinuing medications, always discuss with your doctor.

Medications can sometimes be compounded to prevent them from having illegal ingredients; we have Nystatin for one of my children compounded to only include the drug, water, and stevia. I just have to shake it up before giving it to her.

Supplements:

We will discontinue most supplements for at least the first week, even fermented cod liver oil.

I will re-introduce cod liver oil when 'fermented fish' is allowed in the 2nd stage of the introduction diet.

We also will discontinue B12 injections, even though that bypasses the digestive tract.

We will continue digestive enzymes because the intro diet is very high in fat, which my little one has been shown not to digest well on her own.

Coffee:

I have successfully quit coffee with the amino acid DLPA, which helps the body stop addictive behaviors.

Needed Kitchen Equipment

As with food, it pays to have the highest quality kitchen equipment that you can afford.

Needed kitchen equipment:

I found that I use different kitchen equipment for following a grain free diet than I did with a diet based on grains. Here are some things that I have found useful:

- 8-quart Calphalon Stainless Stockpot- for stock, this one is nice quality, which is so appreciated since it is used every day!
- Slow Cooker: Perfect for cooking stews and soups overnight or when out of the house all day.
- Immersion blender: To puree soups right in the pot.
- Food Processor: With the slicing disks this makes slicing vegetables for

ferments go so much faster. I use my food processor much more often than my stand mixer when we are on GAPS. Not only is it great for vegetables, but it is prefect for mixing coconut flour into baked goods evenly later down the line, making mayonnaise, and pureeing sauces, and even making nutbutter.
- Decent quality blender: I know some people swear by the higher quality blenders, but I haven't found the need for one yet, I like that it has a glass pitcher and metal-on-metal fittings.
- Salt and pepper grinders: Course sea salt is unrefined and contains trace minerals that are so essential from the sea. Freshly ground black pepper is so much more flavorful than pre-ground and is a wonderful addition to meals.
- Wide Mouth Mason jars - Half gallon, quart, pint. Half gallon and quarts are used for yogurt, chicken stock. Pints are used for just about everything else; mayonnaise, dressings, ferments, leftovers, even as drinking glasses.
- Dehydrator: I love my Excalibur dehydrator for its ease of use, temperature control, and quality. In the introduction diet we would not use it much unless you are making 24-hour yogurt, but later on when you can have jerky, dried fruits, and crispy nuts it is indispensible. Also excellent for dehydrating the abundance of summer produce to add to soups in the winter.
- Nice knives. I recommend JA Henckles knives, at the least a chef's knife and paring knife.
- Wide mouth thermoses, perfect for packing soup with veggies and meat. The Thermos brand that I have comes with a spoon that fits nicely right in the lid.
- Garlic Press. You can also puree garlic in a food processor and add a bit of olive oil, and then keep in the fridge for a week or so to use that way.

What Could Go Wrong? (The Healing Crisis)

Familiarize yourself potential 'side effects' of GAPS Intro.

This is my opinion only and cannot be considered medical advice. Please check with your doctor.

Symptoms of Low Carb

I personally have had bad experiences when my diet gets too low in carbohydrate, and I choose not to allow my diet to get so low in carbs that it affects me. Ketosis comes from a low carbohydrate diet, where the body is running on fat and not carbohydrates. Some people do not react poorly, or they choose to push through the symptoms.

Symptoms of ketosis:

- Excessive thirst
- Excessive urination
- Lightheadedness
- Nausea
- Vomiting
- Loss of desire to eat
- Lethargy
- Headache

How to get out of ketosis:

Increase the amount of carbs immediately, even if you don't feel like eating. This can be done with fruit, juice, dates, or by eating a lot of squash or cooked onions (pureed is easiest).

What we've done:

I accidentally went too low carb a few times when breastfeeding, and both times a cup of juice or apple sauce and a nap had me better in a few hours. My children did well on the Intro diet for the first couple days, but the third and fourth day they didn't eat enough vegetables and they started excessive thirst and urination, so I opted to give them some peeled cooked apples ahead of schedule, and then once they got back on track I took it back out and carried on. The last time I did intro, I was only breastfeeding a couple times a day (a toddler) and was able to avoid any bad symptoms on just the vegetables allowed on the GAPS intro as outlined here.

Die Off

When starting a diet which re-balances the internal ecosystem it means that pathogenic bacteria and yeast are going to die. That's our goal! To get rid of the bad and bring in the good. But during this, 'die off' can occur. Die off is when the bad bugs die, and release their toxins as they do so. Our goal should be to not get rid of them as quickly as possible, but to gently detoxify and replenish with good bacteria. If you are feeling die off symptoms (headache, fatigue, aches, digestive upset) you may want to try to slow down the detoxification to a more manageable amount. This can be done by eliminating or using less cultured foods, eliminating coconut oil, and even doing GAPS in stages- first go gluten free, then to full GAPS, then down to intro GAPS.

1 Week Before: Purchase Meat as Needed

One Week Before

Order meat if needed. You can order from US Wellness Meats. The following are my recommendations:

- Chicken backs for making stock when you have too much meat
- Whole chickens for stock and meat if your family eats lots of meat
- Chicken liver
- Beef liver
- Lamb
- Lamb tallow

- Beef tallow
- Lamb
- Beef

Purchase fish if needed- check locally, I couldn't find an online retailer that had everything. If you know any fishermen, they may have extra as well- many people enjoy the sport of fishing more than the eating of the fish.

- Wild caught fish, including heads, bones, and skin (trout, cod)
- Fish roe, wild caught

Evaluate Personal Care Products

Evaluate what toiletries you will need to replace with natural alternatives.

- Make deodorant
- Purchase natural shampoo
- (plain apple cider vinegar, just on the ends, works as a great rinse)
- Purchase natural soap
- Switch to natural makeup
- Make homemade salve/lotion
- Switch to a natural tooth paste, tooth soap, or just plain water for brushing
- Stock your bathroom with canisters of what is needed for detox baths.

Natural deodorant

5 or so tablespoons coconut oil

¾ cup baking soda

15 drops of rosemary (or any type) essential oil

Melt the coconut oil, add in the baking soda and rosemary. Spoon into an empty deodorant container, or into your other lidded container of choice. Will set up as it cools. I've found this to be very effective, though take care when applying when wearing dark shirts.

Detox Baths

Detox baths are a part of the GAPS intro (and continuing) protocol. You will alternate between seaweed, Epsom salt, apple cider vinegar, and baking soda. Seaweed powder can be purchased at Mountain Rose Herbs.

All Purpose Salve

In a double boiler over simmering water melt 2 ounces of pure beeswax (I found mine at our farmer's market for $1/oz or it's available from Mountain Rose Herbs)

Remove from heat and add in 14-16 ounces of coconut oil; I used raw extra virgin for it's antibacterial properties.

The heat from the water will melt the coconut oil easily, but not heating it so hot that you lose the properties associated with raw coconut oil. Coconut oil melts above 76 degrees, so that's all we need to raise it up to.

If desired, mix in 30 drops of an essential oil of your choice- I used lavendar. At this point you can add powdered herbs to make the salve more therapeutic, but I opted to just keep it plain and all purpose.

Stir with a fork to evenly distribute the essential oil, beeswax, and coconut oil and pour into a lidded container to cool (cool with the lid on or off, it doesn't matter). Pour into a lidded container to store. Keeps at room temperature.

Start Cultured Vegetables

Fermented food is an important part of the GAPS Intro diet. It introduces good bacteria into the gut.

Start fermented vegetables:

- Kimchi
- Sauerkraut
- Pickles

Try to purchase organic vegetables for the ferments, even if you have to use conventional produce in the soups.

Kimchi

1 Napa cabbage

1 bunch of Green onions

3 Carrots

1 bunch of Radishes

1 tablespoon fresh Ginger, grated

4 cloves of Garlic

4 chili peppers (mild or spicy, depending on your taste preference)

4 teaspoons sea salt

1 teaspoon Whey per mason jar (optional)

Aside from the ginger and carrots, which you might want to grate smaller, thinly slice all the vegetables and mix with the salt. Place into jars, pounding down to release juice. Add whey over the top, cover with a lid, and set in a room temperature place to ferment for 2-3 days without opening (I leave mine in the basement so they're off my counter top, but I've left my ferments on my counter many times). Transfer to fridge after that and enjoy now or later. Left unopened, my ferments last months in my fridge, but once you open them and use within a couple weeks.

Pickles

Ingredients:

A dozen or so small pickling cucumbers, or 3 large cucumbers cut into spears.

2 teaspoons unrefined sea salt per jar

2 teaspoons mustard seed

2 teaspoons dried dill

Filtered water

Directions:

Wash cucumbers. The small cucumbers can stay whole. Pack into half gallon or quart sized wide mouth mason jars, as many as you need. The pickles can be packed tightly. Distribute the mustard seed and dill among the jars, add filtered water to within ½ inch of the top, and add 2 teaspoons of sea salt (coarse salt is fine) and any amount of optional ferment juice to each jar. Screw on an airtight lid tightly. Place in a cool room temperature place to ferment for 3-4 days, testing one jar to see if pickles are sufficiently sour. Move all jars to the fridge; unopened they keep for months, use within a couple weeks after opening.

I find fermenting pickles at a cooler room temperature makes crisper pickles.

Sauerkraut

Ingredients:

1 head cabbage, green or purple

2 tablespoons sea salt, course is fine

2 quart sized large mouth mason jars

Food processor or knife

Cup or cylinder that fits inside the mason jar, to smash sauerkraut

Directions:

Remove and discard outer leaves of the cabbage, until you get to the clean unblemished leaves underneath. Cut cabbage in half and core. Shred cabbage in food processor using a 'slicing' disk or with a knife, creating thin strips of cabbage. Pack into jars, and add 1 tablespoon salt to each jar. Cover and shake to distribute the salt. Allow to sit out for an hour, until the cabbage wilts. Smash to release juices. Cover again, and allow to ferment on counter for 3 days before transferring to the fridge to store. Sauerkraut is ready to eat after the countertop fermentation.

1-2 Days Before Starting: Make Chicken Stock

Chicken stock is essential for providing the gut with needed amino acids, vitamins, minerals, and fats needed to heal.

1-2 Days Before starting

- Thaw Chicken
- Make Chicken Stock

Chicken stock:

Ingredients

Whole chicken or chicken pieces

Optional: 2 tablespoons thyme, 6 cloves garlic, 1 onion, 1 inch of ginger root, vegetable scraps such as the ends of onions and carrots, core of the cabbage, leaves from celery, etc

Directions:

Rinse chicken. Reach inside cavity and remove giblet package. Remove giblets from package and add to the stock pot. Place chicken in the stockpot.

Fill pot ¾ full with filtered water and any optional herbs and vegetables. Cook on medium-high until bubbling, then reduce heat to low and allow to simmer, covered, at least 8 hours. When done, allow to cool then pour stock through a strainer and transfer to mason jars to store in the fridge.

To strain, I use a mesh strainer over a pitcher-style 4-cup measuring cup. This makes transferring the stock to the mason jars easier; I do one jar at a time, cleaning out the strainer as needed during the process.

Do not discard the soft gelatinous parts around the bones or the skin; reserve that and use an immersion or regular blender to blend it into your stock and soups.

The fat will rise to the top of the jars in the fridge, which can be included in soups or used as a fat for cooking.

Pick any meat off the bones that you can after the chicken stock has been removed, reserve meat to add to soups or serve alongside. Discard the remaining bones in the pot.

Veggie Prep

Bulk Food Preparation

Preparing vegetables ahead of time can make the work of starting GAPS seem much less overwhelming. Prepared vegetables can be frozen in ziplock or glass containers.

Purchase:

- 6-12 large butternut squash or other winter squash
- 6 leeks
- 1 bunch green onions
- 10 pounds white or yellow onions
- 3 heads broccoli (3 pounds organic frozen can be used)
- 3 heads cauliflower (3 pounds organic frozen can be used)
- Fresh herbs: basil, dill, thyme, sage, rosemary
- 3-5 heads garlic

Prepare:

- Peel butternut squash, cut off neck and cut neck into 'squash fries' – fry shapes. Scoop out pulp from bulb, and chop into chunks for adding to soup, boiling, and mashing.
- Wash, remove ends, and thinly slice leeks.
- Chop broccoli florets, reserving stems in a separate bag to add to stock as desired.
- Chop cauliflower florets, reserving stems for stock if desired.
- Rinse herbs, pat dry, and remove from stems. Freeze to crumble into soups.
- Peel garlic, freeze without crushing; garlic can be crushed with a garlic press without thawing.

{Tip} Picky Eaters, Sensory Issues, and the GAPS Diet

"Eggs? Meat? Nuts? All my child will eat is bread and ketchup"

"He's a picky eater. He'd starve"

"It's genetic, our family is full of picky eaters, she would never eat the GAPS food"

"It's the textures… the only thing he will swallow is pureed food"

Yep, I understand. Many "GAPS Kids" or as I refer to them while talking with other parents who have special needs children, 'our kids,' have very strong likes and dislikes with food, and we can already feel like we're battling to get them to eat our favorites. I just wrote a post about how I get my kids to eat and this works well for our family now, after years of the GAPS (Gut and

Psychology Syndrome) diet and years of understanding her quirks and what wording or situations encourage or discourage her to eat healthy food.

So, how do I introduce the GAPS Diet with my special needs child?

1. I'm a mom, not a medical professional, before changing your child's diet you should run it by qualified professionals.
2. After you've done that, I recommend slowly removing things from their diet. We were already dairy free when my little one was 2-1/2, so we next took out gluten. There are lots of child friendly gluten free casein free foods on the market now, so you most likely can find gluten free alternatives to what your child currently is eating.
3. Going gluten free can cause a healing crisis, so allow your child to become completely comfortable gluten free before pushing it any more.
4. Try different GAPS foods and see if any of them are enjoyed by your child, and gradually increase those as you can, while continuing the GFCF. See my GAPS Recipes page for ideas.
5. Introduce probiotic containing foods like homemade sauerkraut and probiotic supplements if desired. These also can trigger healing crises so watch carefully.
6. Next, go down to full GAPS, which is grain and refined sugar free. This could cause a rebellion, since when you pull the rest of the foods that are feeding the bad gut flora, the brain is flooded with messages that this diet is NOT what the bacteria want (see It's the Bacteria Talking, below)
7. And then finally try the GAPS Introduction diet. The Intro diet is so so healing and helpful, but jumping right in is a big change for many kids.

Desperate parents have tried jumping to Intro right away, and saw great benefits for it, but if you can try a more gradual approach, this is what we did and I feel it worked well. The previous steps took us about 10 weeks, so it's not too too long, and we saw results with every step.

Wouldn't it work to just not give in?

Nope. You can't just put a plate of GAPS food in front of a child that has previously only eaten a very limited range of foods and expect them to finally give up and just eat it, it's not a discipline issue, it's a sensory issue. This advice might have worked for well meaning grandparents with typically developing children, but with GAPS kids this is a sensory issue – and they literally will starve themselves to the point of harm rather than eat a food they don't find suitable.

It's the bacteria talking

In the gut-brain connection post we talked about how bad gut flora can give off toxins that affect our brains like drugs. That's what this sensitivity to textures and tastes is all about, in the same way our body tells us to avoid bitter foods because they likely are poisonous our kids with sensory issues are being 'told' that this food is not good to eat. That's what makes picky eaters when it comes to sensory issues.

Give it just 7 days

The good thing about it being a gut flora issue is that it's generally easily corrected! After just a week on the GAPS diet, or even gluten free, many kids are eating many more foods. I commonly get emails from parents that tell me that after a week on GAPS their 4 year old is happily eating tons of squash, soup, meat, and eggs- all foods that had been disliked in the past.

For the 3-7 days that you're starting the diet, I wouldn't worry about anything other than only limiting your child to GAPS approved foods. Even if they will only eat apple sauce for days, this often starves out enough of the bad gut flora that they can then tolerate more GAPS foods.

Your job during this time is to make sure they're not getting any cheats at all- even a crumb of bread or couple grains of rice at this stage will feed the bad gut flora and prevent them from dying off, and all your hard work will be negated. Watch for sugar or additives in supplements, and get different versions if they have offending ingredients. GAPS, especially in the beginning, isn't something you can do 80% or even 99%, it requires 100% adherence to be successful. After the gut has healed quite a bit (this was after about a year for us) occasional cheats won't mess the GAPS person up so much, but at the beginning it's mandatory to be strict.

Jump Starting Eating and Other Behavior Techniques

Even though starting GAPS will help considerably with eating new foods, parenting techniques can still help our children eat healthily. My little one has a combination of being easily overstimulated visually (lights, colors, movement), and under-stimulated with sound and touch/pressure. If any of these are out of balance, or if she's overly hungry or tired she has a harder time focusing on eating, and this being hungry can just add to her being overwhelmed and inability to focus on eating.

To break the cycle if we get into it, I will do anything I can to get her to eat a few bites of food. Usually once she's eaten a few bites she sees how good that feels, and will continue eating. To get the first few bites in, I often sit her on my lap (still! She's 6!), put one arm behind my back, hold the other hand, and put a bite of whatever she's most likely to eat from my plate in her mouth.

Another thing that works for her is to make a silly, loud, energetic game with it. Yes, I'll still do the 'airplane' game with buzzing the fork around in the air, she enjoys it, I enjoy it, and it's meeting her developmentally where she is at that moment.

Some parents have reported success letting kids do their favorite activity, and building taking a bite of food into it as a game. For example, the child might love stairs, so encourage them to walk up 3 stairs, and then in a happy encouraging voice say '3 stairs, then a bite, here you go, then 3 more stairs!'. Opening doors is a big one for us, we have used that to get her to do what she needs to do in the past too, "Open, shut, bite! Open, shut, bite!". When doing diet therapies, it's really important to just get the kids to eat however we can. Once we're a few days or weeks in, it becomes so much easier, I promise.

For some children the 'when, then' approach works well. My daughter didn't like that, but this is what's described in the GAPS book and works for many parents. The diet is started by allowing one bite of favored food (any food, even non GAPS food) after a bite of GAPS food (soup, meat, etc) is eaten. This way the child gets used to the taste of the GAPS food, and slowly is weaned off the favored foods.

Start Young

When we have toddlers with special needs, it looks like it might be easier to wait and start when the children can talk and reason. I personally advocate you start as soon as possible. When we started I could easily prevent my child from accessing foods that weren't on the diet by putting them high in the pantry, putting a latch on the fridge, or just not having them available in the house. The older kids get, the more independent they are and the more access they have to illegal foods, and during the start of GAPS when the bad gut flora are dying off and sending chemicals to the brain that says you *need* bread, sugar, and grains, it's really hard to have that much self control as an adult, much less a child.

Set a time period, a start date, and go!

When we started GAPS, I decided to start Nov 1, 2009, and we would try it for 30 days. That gave me the motivation to give it a good try. We obviously found it worth it to continue the diet, but getting through the first week was the hardest.

{Tip} Activities You Can Do That Don't Revolve Around Food

Activities You Can Do That Don't Revolve Around Food

It's great to keep busy and out of the house especially on the introduction diet. Being near the kitchen or in the grocery store can be distracting.

To follow are some ideas that we enjoy- you may find some of them helpful for distracting and keeping busy.

This list of ideas will also be helpful for getting together with friends. People typically have social gatherings at coffee shops, fast food play areas, and over meals. When following a special diet, it's often easier to just bypass the whole food thing altogether and meet somewhere else.

Ideas:

- Taking walks
- Visiting 'far away' parks rather than just the one in your neighborhood
- Digging in the sand if there is a nearby beach or river
- Coloring with crayons
- 'Wax resist' using watercolors over crayon drawing
- Using markers and coloring 'fuzzy posters'
- Drawing or painting on butcher paper
- Collecting natural play things: stumps, pinecones, sticks
- Watching airplanes if you have a nearby airport
- Bubbles
- Zoo
- Biking
- Hiking
- Modeling Clay
- Building projects: simple shelf, bird house
- Planting and tending a garden
- Puppet shows
- Origami
- Sewing/quilting

{Tip} What Should I Say to Others?

What Should I Say to Others?

Starting a diet like GAPS, especially the more restrictive Intro GAPS can make for awkward conversations. I didn't realize how much of our every day 'small talk' revolved around food and health problems until we started going down the unconventional natural medicine path! I don't like to make waves, so I do try to minimize food talk as much as possible when I'm around people I know will not agree with what we're doing.

This is what I have come up with for situations that present as my family has been on a restricted diet.

Family and Friends

If we are planning a visit, be it for 20 minutes or 2 weeks, with family or friends, I do my best to warn them ahead of time that we're following a temporary diet change right now, so our family/the kids can't eat anything other than what I give them. If the people are interested, I explain as much as I think they'd like to hear- I love to talk about GAPS and natural health! If not, I talk minimally, but do try to get the point across that absolutely nothing can be eaten other than the food I have prepared. This helps avoid hurt feelings or embarrassment over offered food.

If people are concerned, I stress that it is a temporary diet and we will discontinue it either if it turns out to not be effective, and/or when it is no longer needed. I have no problem calling the diet 'crazy' or 'ridiculous' as a way to take the pressure off the situation and laugh about it together.

Those who invite us to eat at their house

As kindly and graciously as possible, I tell friends that I would love to, but we are following a restricted diet right now for some health issues, so to enjoy their company I'd love to get together to do something not food related instead, or meet for a bring-your-own-food picnic.

I try not to go into what we can or cannot eat, if a well-meaning friend prepares a meal that contains illegal ingredients (the GAPS protocols can be hard for someone not familiar with the diet to follow!) that would be harder to deal with than avoiding the food altogether.

Some fun family friendly alternatives: Card games, visiting a park, swimming in a lake, fishing, hiking, bowling, going to the movies, taking a class, are all fun activities that others can join.

At social functions

At church, scout meetings, class parties, etc, food is nearly always present! To avoid misshaps, I personally don't leave my children, even with people who appear to understand the dietary restrictions. People forget or don't understand the instructions- I have caught people at church about to hand my child otter pops, candy, crackers, cookies, doughnuts, etc. on many occasions! Each time they 'didn't think there was anything in it', or they mistake the GAPS diet for avoiding allergens like peanuts. I find it's easier to just keep my children with me unless I'm sure that my children have the ability and will to follow the diet even around other food.

Doctors

Most mainstream doctors are not interested in dietary intervention- it wasn't what they learned about in school, and so they often feel threatened by it. I do point out that the GAPS diet is written by Dr. Campbell-McBride, a Neurologist. That helps. When we go to appointments, I will note that we are on a restricted diet, and I'll often photocopy the front of the GAPS book for the doctor's reference and to stick in the chart.

If a doctor disagrees, I 'smile and nod' and assure them I will look into the concerns when I get home, or write down their recommendations for supplements to 'look into' when I get home.

I find it easier to agree to disagree with medical professionals, and stick to the topic that is the reason for the appointment.

Therapists

Many of the children on the GAPS diet are involved with occupational, speech, and physical therapies. I let our therapists know that my child is on a restrictive diet, and that she is chemical sensitive and cannot use hand sanitizer, regular soaps, shaving creams, etc. I let them know that if anything is necessary for therapy, I can find an alternative.

Until I am sure that the therapist will remember not to use chemicals on my child, and they will remember not to offer him candy or other food that isn't allowed, I stay in the therapy appointments. I realize this may not always be possible for every family, but it is what we've done so far.

My children

What to tell the kids… This will vary based on your child, your family, and your parenting style. I can tell you some of the phrases that are used at my house, but they may not work with your family, so you may need to come up with different ways of talking about the GAPS diet with your children. Also, my children are just beginning to talk, so this is more geared towards toddlers.

When my children ask for food allowed on the GAPS diet but not allowed in the intro part, I tell them they can have it 'in a few weeks' or 'after we eat mostly soup this month' and be sure to be positive about some aspect of the food they will be eating, whether it's 'you can use your new thermos!' or 'we'll take our soup to the zoo, wouldn't that be fun?'.

If they ask for something not allowed on GAPS at all, I just tell them 'no, we're not going to have that, that would make you sick'. This isn't a lie- as parents, we are doing GAPS for our children both for their physical and mental health; eczema, ADD, allergies, tummy aches, and general crankiness all can be included in the simple phrase 'sick'.

My personality is both very direct and very optimistic, and I find that this has worked well with getting my children to accept the diet. I also did the diet along with them, and praised the goodness of all the GAPS food. By smiling at my children and encouraging them to talk about the GAPS food they enjoy, the focus is kept on the good part of the meals and meal times are a lovely experience. If I set the tone for the meal with 'Oooo, cauliflower with salt- I LOVE cauliflower, do you LOVE cauliflower?' my little one will often take my lead, or they will retort back with something like 'No, I no love cauliflower, I love MEAT!" J If no food on the GAPS diet is particularly loved, you can still keep the conversation positive by noting the beautiful flower arrangement or candle in the center of the table or talking about fun things that happened that day.

Older children will be able to understand how there are both good bugs and bad bugs in their gut, and we are trying to win the war against the bad bugs.

When To Move To The Next Intro Stage

How do I Know When It's Time to Move to The Next Stage on the GAPS Intro?

Dr. Natasha recommends moving through intro quickly, and trying new foods and watching for reactions. If necessary due to reactions, go back to the previous stage for a few days/week and then try again. Some individuals dealing with things like seizure disorders, autism, and sever digestion issues may need to stay on some stages longer than others. Personally, I was able to heal my milk allergy just running through the introduction diet quickly, in about 4 weeks.

My daughter, on the other hand, has been stuck on stage 5 since the last time we did the Intro diet. Every time I try to introduce honey or fruit, her ADD symptoms return.

Symptoms can be behavioral or physical, watch for anything that went away and then comes back including:

- Diarrhea
- Constipation
- Impulsivity
- Brain Fog
- Tiredness
- Headaches
- Upset Stomach
- Eczema
- Yeast rashes
- Aggressive behavior
- Depression
- Loss of eye contact (and other autism symptoms)
- Stimming (another autism symptom)

Stage 1

Stage 1

You can eat on stage 1:

- Meat or fish stock
- Well boiled broccoli, cauliflower, carrots, onions, leeks
- Squash, winter and summer
- Boiled meat
- Sea salt,
- 1-2 teaspoons a day of sauerkraut juice

Day 1

While on the GAPS Intro, be prepared to eat often as your body adjusts to this super digestible food. The same foods can be served throughout the day to minimize cooking and clean up.

- **Morning Mineral Water**

Upon waking, drink 1 cup of mineral or filtered water. Allow to rest before eating.

Intro Butternut Squash Soup

2 quarts stock

1 quart filtered water

4 cups pre-cut butternut squash cubes

1 tablespoon sea salt (adjust to taste)

Simmer all ingredients to make a soup. Puree with an immersion blender if desired for a smooth soup.

Boiled Broccoli

Simmer 2-4 cups of broccoli until soft. Sprinkle with sea salt, top with the fat that rose to the top of your chicken stock.

Sweet Onions

6-8 small onions

1 quart stock

1 teaspoon sea salt

Simmer small peeled whole onions in enough stock to cover for one hour, covered, until soft all the way through. Reserve leftover stock for soup.

Chicken meat with Soup

Gently heat chicken left from stock in a steamer or by boiling in water. Top with Butternut squash soup, or dip in the soup.

Recipes in this guide serve 4 people. Due to the vast differences in the amount people are hungry for on the Intro diet, you may find that you don't need all the food on each day. Look at the recipes from the current day, and the previous days, and see what sounds good and then cook from there.

When we were on intro I ate mostly soups, my toddler son ate almost exclusively meat, and my preschooler daughter ate mostly veggies and a little meat. Within the allowed foods, choices and quantities will be very individual.

Detox Bath:

1 cup Epsom salt

Include Day 1:

o Broth with every meal
o Soup at least one meal
o Crushed garlic in soup right before eating
o Detox Bath

Day 2

What is the difference between a food intolerance and a just an off day or hormone fluctuations?

Often it's hard to tell whether less noticeable symptoms (fatigue, moodiness, slight headaches) are from introducing a new food or are from just having poor sleep the night before, starting your menstrual cycle, or even a change in the weather. In this case, I normally give the new food 3 days, if the symptoms haven't subsided, then I'll go ahead and pull the food out again. Your results may vary, but this is how I approach mild symptoms.

Recipes:

- **Morning Mineral Water**

Upon waking, drink 1 cup of mineral or filtered water. Allow to rest before eating.

Meat Patties

3 pounds hamburger

3 carrots and 1 cup cauliflower, shredded

2 cups stock

½ teaspoon sea salt

Form hamburger into patties, simmer in stock with the vegetables until cooked through. Blend the veggies into the stock after removing the patties, and serve as a 'sauce' over the top.

Meat Strips

1 roast, 4 pounds

2 quarts water

1 teaspoon sea salt

Slice roast into 'jerky' like strips, and simmer meat strips in water with salt for 30 minutes or until cooked through.

Onion Leek Soup

2 quarts stock

1 quart water

5 onions, sliced

4 leeks, sliced

2 cloves garlic, crushed

1 tablespoon sea salt (or to taste)

Simmer everything for one hour or overnight on low in the crockpot.

Squash chunks

4 cups squash chunks

4 tablespoons animal fat (lamb, beef, chicken, etc)

Sprinkle of sea salt

In a saucepan with a lid, simmer squash in enough water to cover for 30 minutes, or until very soft. Drain gently and top with fat and salt.

Detox Bath:

1 cup Baking Soda

Include:

o Broth with every meal

o Soup at least one meal

o Crushed garlic in soup right before eating

o Detox Bath

Detox Bath:

1 cup Baking Soda

Day 3

Recipes:

- **Morning Mineral Water**

Upon waking, drink 1 cup of mineral or filtered water. Allow to rest before eating.

Fish Stock

2 pounds fish with bones and scales.

Filtered water

Directions: Simmer whole fish in water for 8 hours. Strain meat and bones. Set meat aside to add to soup, store broth as needed in mason jars.

Creamy Cauliflower

2 pounds cauliflower

1 quart stock

½ teaspoon salt

4 tablespoons lamb tallow

Boil cauliflower until soft, 20 minutes. Drain, reserving stock for use in soup. "Butter" the cauliflower with tallow and sprinkle with salt.

Boiled Steak:

Boil 6-8 steaks, sprinkle with salt.

Crockpot Onions

1 quart stock

1 quart water

1 teaspoon salt

8 onions, peeled (whole)

Peel as many onions as will fit in your crockpot- about 8. Add a quart of stock and 1 teaspoon of sea salt and cook on low all day or overnight.

Mashed Carrots

8 carrots

Filtered water

1 teaspoon sea salt

2 tablespoons tallow

2 garlic cloves, crushed

Peel and simmer the carrots and garlic in water with salt. Once soft (1 hour or so) drain and mash, adding the tallow.

> *Fish stock is rich in minerals and essential fatty acids. If your family likes, it it's a great base for stocks, if they don't, keep it in jars in the fridge and add 1-4 cups per batch of soup made with chicken and beef stock, which is often preferred.*

Prepare:

Beef Stock:

Beef marrow bones

Filtered water

In a crockpot or stock pot, place 1-2 pounds beef marrow bones and fill to 1 inch from the top with filtered water. Simmer overnight. If there is meat on your stock bones, pull meat off and save for later use.

Introduce:

1 teaspoon sauerkraut juice

Detox Bath:

1 cup apple cider vinegar

Include:

o Fermented sauerkraut juice

o Broth with every meal

o Soup at least one meal

o Crushed garlic in soup before eating

o Detox Bath

Day 4

Recipes:

- **Morning Mineral Water**

Upon waking, drink 1 cup of mineral or filtered water. Allow to rest before eating.

Beef and Broccoli Soup

2 quarts beef stock

1-2 cups fish stock (*optional*)

1 quart filtered water

1 tablespoon sea salt (to taste)

2 cloves garlic, peeled and crushed

2 pounds broccoli

2 pounds beef roast, or meat from stock bones if your bones came with meat like mine do.

In a crockpot or in a stockpot combine stock, water, salt, garlic, and broccoli. Simmer 1 hour

Or until broccoli is very soft. Blend with an immersion blender until smooth. Add back in beef and heat until warm, or chop a beef roast into bite sized pieces and simmer until cooked through.

Boiled Squash

Boil bite sized squash pieces until soft. Top with tallow and salt.

Simmered Chicken and Acorn Squash

2 pounds chicken, chopped, or chicken picked off of the chicken used for stock.

2 pounds butternut squash, peeled and chopped

1 teaspoon sea salt

Simmer chicken pieces with butternut squash pieces

Chicken stock:

Whole chicken or chicken pieces

Directions:

Rinse chicken. Reach inside cavity and remove giblet package. Remove giblets from package and add to the stock pot. Place chicken in the stockpot.

Fill pot ¾ full with filtered water. Cook on medium-high until bubbling, then reduce heat to low and allow to simmer, covered, at least 8 hours. When done, allow to cool then pour stock through a strainer and transfer to mason jars to store in the fridge.

Strain and pour stock into jars.

Do not discard the soft gelatinous parts around the bones or the skin; reserve that and use an immersion or regular blender to blend it into your stock and soups.

The fat will rise to the top of the jars in the fridge, which can be included in soups or used as a fat for cooking.

Pick any meat off the bones that you can after the chicken stock has been removed, reserve meat to add to soups or serve alongside. Discard the remaining bones in the pot.

Introduce: Increase sauerkraut juice if tolerated.

Seaweed Detox Bath:

The GAPS book isn't very specific about what seaweed is used in the detox bath. I have found kelp powder to be the easiest to clean out of my tub (it goes down the drain and can be rinsed off the sides with the shower head) and due to the cost, many people choose to just use a couple tablespoons per bath.

Dulse or other seaweed flakes can also be tied up in a mesh or muslin bag and steeped in the bath as a mess-free 'tea'

Detox Bath:

1 cup Seaweed Powder

Include:

o Fermented sauerkraut juice

o Broth with every meal

o Soup at least one meal

o Crushed garlic in soup at the end

o Detox Bath

Day 5

Recipes:

Morning Mineral Water

Upon waking, drink 1 cup of mineral or filtered water. Allow to rest before eating.

Boiled Meatballs with carrots and onions

3 pounds ground meat

1 carrot

1 onion

½ teaspoon sea salt

Puree or grate carrot and onion, mix with meat and salt and form into balls. Simmer in stock or water. Reserve water or stock from simmering to add for soup.

Garlic Tip: To easily peel garlic, pull a couple cloves off the head, then crush them with your palm. They will peel easily now and can be added like this since the soup if it will be pureed, or crushed with a press, or diced with a chef's knife.

Boiled Lamb

4 lamb chops

Gently simmer lamb until cooked through. Salt to taste.

Lamb Stock:

Ingredients

Lamb bones

Filtered water

Directions:

Fill pot ¾ full with filtered water, add lamb bones. Cook on medium-high until bubbling, then reduce heat to low and allow to simmer, covered, at least 8 hours. When done, allow to cool then pour stock through a strainer and transfer to mason jars to store in the fridge.

Summer Squash Soup

2 quarts stock

1 quart filtered water

8 small summer squash; crookneck, zucchini, patty pan, etc

1 tablespoon sea salt (adjust to taste)

Remove stems and blossom ends from squash, coarsely chop. Simmer all ingredients to make a soup. Puree with an immersion blender if desired for a smooth soup.

Detox Bath:

1 cup Epsom salt

Include:

o Fermented sauerkraut juice

o Broth with every meal

o Soup at least one meal

o Crushed garlic in soup at the end

o Detox Bath

Stage 2

Stage 2

You can eat on Stage 2:

- Meat or fish stock
- Well boiled GAPS-legal vegetables (no starchy root vegetables)
- Squash, winter and summer
- Boiled meat
- Sea salt
- Fresh herbs
- Fermented vegetables; sauerkraut, kimchi, pickles
- Fermented fish
- Egg yolk, organic, carefully separated from the white
- Homemade ghee
- Stews and casseroles made with meat and vegetables

Day 6

Recipes:

Morning Mineral Water

Upon waking, drink 1 cup of mineral or filtered water. Allow to rest before eating.

Butternut Squash and Beef Casserole

2 pounds hamburger

1 large butternut squash (3 pounds)

½ teaspoon sea salt

2 cups stock

Tallow or fat to grease pan

Preheat oven to 350* Mix hamburger with sea salt. Peel and remove pulp from butternut squash, and chop into bite-sized pieces. Grease a 9x13" pan with fat. Place squash in the pan and pour stock over the squash. Place pieces of the raw hamburger over the top of the squash, covering evenly. Bake uncovered for 45 minutes or until squash is soft and beef is cooked.

Creamy Cauliflower

2 pounds cauliflower

1 quart stock

½ teaspoon salt

4 tablespoons lamb tallow

Boil cauliflower until soft, 20 minutes. Drain, reserving stock for use in soup. "Butter" the cauliflower with tallow and sprinkle with salt.

> *Stage 2 allows more foods, but try to introduce them one at a time so that you are sure what you're tolerating and what you're not.*

Intro Butternut Squash Soup

2 quarts stock

1 quart filtered water

4 cups pre-cut butternut squash cubes

1 tablespoon sea salt (adjust to taste)

Simmer all ingredients to make a soup. Puree with an immersion blender if desired for a smooth soup.

Beef Stock:

Beef marrow bones

Filtered water

In a crockpot or stock pot, place beef marrow bones and fill to 1 inch from the top with filtered water. Simmer overnight.

Introduce:

Start with 1 teaspoon fermented vegetable; kimchi or sauerkraut.

Detox Bath:

1 cup Baking Soda

Include:

o Fermented sauerkraut juice

- Fermented vegetable

o Broth with every meal

o Soup at least one meal

o Crushed garlic in soup at the end

o Detox Bath

Day 7

Recipes:

- **Morning Mineral Water**

Upon waking, drink 1 cup of mineral or filtered water. Allow to rest before eating.

Zucchini casserole

2 pounds chicken, cubed

4 zucchinis

1 teaspoon sea salt

½ cup stock

Cube chicken in bite sized pieces. Slice zucchini into ¼ inch rounds. Place chicken and stock in the bottom of a loaf pan, sprinkle with salt, and top with zucchini rounds. Cover with foil and bake at 350* for 45 minutes, or until chicken is cooked through and zucchini is soft.

Creamy Summer Squash Soup

2 quarts stock

1 quart filtered water

8 small summer squash ;crookneck, zucchini, patty pan, etc

1 tablespoon sea salt (adjust to taste)

Remove stems and blossom ends from squash, coarsely chop. Simmer all ingredients to make a soup. Puree with an immersion blender. Serve, allow to cool slightly and then add one raw egg yolk, carefully separated from the white. Stir gently with a fork and enjoy!

Re-ferment cabbage as needed

If you have used up the juice from your sauerkraut but are still using quite a bit, you can add 1 teaspoon of sea salt and 1 cup of water to your previously fermented sauerkraut, and allow to sit out on the counter again for 2-3 days to re-ferment.

Egg yolks make for very creamy nutrient rich soups and are introduced today!

Introduce:

Carefully separated egg yolk, one stirred into each bowl of soup

Detox Bath:

1 cup apple cider vinegar

Include:

o Fermented sauerkraut juice or vegetables

o Broth with every meal

o Soup at least one meal

o Egg yolks in soup

o Crushed garlic in soup at the end

o **Detox Bath**

Day 8

Recipes:

Morning Mineral Water

Upon waking, drink 1 cup of mineral or filtered water. Allow to rest before eating.

Smooth Carrot Soup with Squash and Garlic

5-10 large carrots, scrubbed

6 small to medium summer squash

4 cloves garlic, peeled and minced

2 quarts stock

1 tablespoon sea salt (to taste)

Filtered water

Chop carrots and squash and place in pot. Add stock, salt, and then add water to fill pot or crock pot. Simmer 2 hours on the stove or cook all day in the crockpot. Add garlic just before serving. Puree with immersion blender and add in meat chunks if desired after pureeing.

Boiled Meatballs with Garlic and Parsley

3 pounds hamburger

3 carrots and 1 cup cauliflower, shredded

3 cloves garlic, minced or crushed

3 sprigs fresh parsley, finely chopped

2 cups stock

½ teaspoon sea salt

Mix hamburger with vegetables, garlic, and parsley. Simmer in stock with added sea salt, gently turning as needed, until cooked through.

Introduce:

Fermented cod liver oil

> Information on cod liver oil starts on page 277 in the GAPS book. The dose recommendation for adults is 1 teaspoon a day to start (go down to ½ teaspoon after a few weeks), ½ teaspoon for children (go down to ¼ teaspoon after a few weeks). Double the adult dose for pregnant or lactating women.

Detox Bath:

1 cup Seaweed Powder

Include:

o Fermented sauerkraut juice or vegetables

o Broth with every meal

o Soup at least one meal

- Cod liver oil

o Egg yolks in soup

o Crushed garlic in soup at the end

o Detox Bath

Day 9

Recipes:

Morning Mineral Water

Upon waking, drink 1 cup of mineral or filtered water. Allow to rest before eating.

Egg Drop Soup

6 leeks, sliced

1 quart fish stock

1 quart other stock

2 teaspoons sea salt

4 onions, sliced

4 egg yolks, beaten with a fork

Wash and slice the leeks up to where the leaves separate (use the light parts) and peel and slice the onions thinly. Simmer in stock with salt until soft, 1 hour. Raise heat to a rapid boil and gently drip in a thin stream of egg yolks, whisking with a fork as you pour them in to make 'noodles'. Remove from heat and serve.

> *I buy my ghee from Pure Indian Foods, but here is directions for making your own if you wish, if you are wary of cow dairy, I have purchased goat milk butter before at our health food store- you may be able to ask yours to carry it too, and use that to make goat milk ghee. See recipe below.*

Homemade ghee

1 pound unsalted butter, or more as desired

Preheat oven to 140-250* Place butter in an oven proof dish or pan. Bake for 45-60 minutes, take out very carefully, and pour the golden fat from the top, being careful to leave the white milk solids in the pan. Keep in a glass jar and refrigerate. You can save the buttery milk solids for others who eat butter in the house, or discard.

Stuffed Peppers

6 bell peppers

1-2 pounds assorted vegetables (carrot, onion, broccoli, cauliflower), shredded

3 pounds ground meat, raw

½ teaspoon sea salt

Mix veggies, meat, and salt. Wash and cut tops off bell peppers, rinse out seeds. Stuff meat evenly into bell peppers. Place in a casserole dish with a lid, add ½ inch water to the bottom. Bake at 350* for one hour covered, or until meat is cooked through and peppers are soft. Serve.

Prepare:

Crispy Walnuts (we will dehydrate them tomorrow):

To soak nuts: Place 2-3 lbs raw nuts in a large bowl (they will swell, so only fill 2/3 full, using another bowl if needed). Add 2 tablespoons sea salt and cover the nuts with filtered water. Allow to soak overnight at room temperature (on the counter). No need to cover.

Detox Bath:

1 cup Epsom salt

Include:

- Fermented sauerkraut juice or vegetables
- Broth with every meal
- Soup at least one meal
  - Cod liver oil
- Egg yolks in soup
- Crushed garlic in soup at the end
- Detox Bath

Day 10

Recipes:

Morning Mineral Water

Upon waking, drink 1 cup of mineral or filtered water. Allow to rest before eating.

Chicken stock:

Ingredients

Whole chicken or chicken pieces

Optional: 2 tablespoons thyme, 6 cloves garlic, 1 onion, 1 inch of ginger root, vegetable scraps such as the ends of onions and carrots, core of the cabbage, leaves from celery, etc

Directions:

Rinse chicken. Reach inside cavity and remove giblet package. Remove giblets from package and add to the stock pot. Place chicken in the stockpot.

Fill pot ¾ full with filtered water and any optional herbs and vegetables. Cook on medium-high until bubbling, then reduce heat to low and allow to simmer, covered, at least 8 hours. When done, allow to cool then pour stock through a strainer and transfer to mason jars to store in the fridge.

Do not discard the soft gelatinous parts around the bones or the skin; reserve that and use an immersion or regular blender to blend it into your stock and soups.

Pick any meat off the bones that you can after the chicken stock has been removed, reserve meat to add to soups or serve alongside. Discard the remaining bones in the pot.

Chunky Chicken Soup

1 pound carrots

1 winter or summer squash, peeled, and cut into cubes

Cooked chicken, cubed

1 quart stock

1 quart filtered water

1 teaspoon sea salt

Simmer chopped veggies in stock and water until soft. Add chicken and heat until warm.

Slow Cooked Pulled Brisket

4 onions or equivalent of other veggies, peeled and sliced

Brisket roast, 3-4 pounds

1 cup stock

½ teaspoon sea salt

In a slow cooker, place sliced onions. Put brisket roast on top and pour stock over. Sprinkle sea salt over roast. Cook on low all day or on high for 4 hours. Remove brisket and puree the onions and stock/drippings into 'gravy' and then place the brisket back in and pull apart with two forks, mixing the gravy in. *(Brisket pictured is topped with olive oil and herbs, allowed later in the introduction diet)*

Prepare:

Crispy Walnuts:

To dry:

Drain in a colander and start dehydrating the nuts you soaked last night, or roast in a pan as low as your oven will go. Dehydrate all day.

Detox Bath:

1 cup Baking Soda

Include:

- o Fermented sauerkraut juice or vegetables

- Broth with every meal
- Soup at least one meal
- Cod liver oil
- Egg yolks in soup
- Crushed garlic in soup at the end
- Detox Bath

Stage 3

Stage 3

You can eat on Stage 3:

- Meat or fish stock
- Well boiled GAPS-legal vegetables (no starchy root vegetables)
- Squash, winter and summer
- Boiled meat
- Sea salt
- Fresh herbs
- Fermented vegetables; sauerkraut, kimchi, pickles
- Fermented fish
- Egg yolk, organic, carefully separated from the white
- Homemade ghee
- Stews and casseroles made with meat and vegetables
- Ripe avocado mashed into soups, starting with 1-3 teaspoons a day
- Pancakes made with nutbutter, squash, and eggs- fried in fat or ghee, start with one a day
- Scrambled eggs made with ghee and served with avocado if tolerated and cooked vegetables.

Day 11

By now I'm sure you are quite excited about the idea of pancakes! Today they are crepes with just egg, to check for tolerance of the whites.

Recipes:

Morning Mineral Water

Upon waking, drink 1 cup of mineral or filtered water. Allow to rest before eating.

Summer Squash Intro Pancakes

1 small crookneck squash

2 eggs

1 teaspoon tallow to fry in

In a blender, blend squash, and eggs until smooth. Heat a skillet on medium-low heat and melt lamb tallow. Make small pancakes with the batter, and carefully flip once set on one side, after 90 seconds or so.

Enjoy!

Intro Broccoli Beef Soup

4 pounds hamburger

2 pounds broccoli

2 pounds cauliflower

2 quarts stock

1 tablespoon sea salt

Simmer all ingredients, breaking up hamburger as it cooks.

Lamb Stock

1-2 pounds lamb marrow bones, broken to allow the marrow to come out

Filtered water

In a large stock pot, place lamb marrow bones. Fill with water to near the top and simmer for 6-8 hours or overnight in the crockpot.

Introduce:

- Egg Whites

Detox Bath:

1 cup apple cider vinegar

Include:

o Fermented sauerkraut juice or vegetables

o Broth with every meal

o Soup at least one meal

- Cod liver oil

o Egg yolks in soup

o Crushed garlic in soup at the end

o Detox Bath

Day 12

Recipes:

Morning Mineral Water

Upon waking, drink 1 cup of mineral or filtered water. Allow to rest before eating.

Lamb and Onion Stew

3-5 pounds lamb, cut into chunks for stew

6 onions, peeled and cut into quarters

6 cloves garlic, diced

2 quarts lamb stock

1 quart filtered water

1 tablespoon sea salt

Simmer onions, lamb, water, stock, and sea salt. Before serving, mince garlic and add to the soup. Serve with kimchi.

Summer Squash Intro Pancakes with Walnuts

1 small crookneck squash or ¼ a butternut squash, peeled and chopped

1 cup crispy walnuts

2 eggs

1 teaspoon tallow to fry in

In a blender, blend squash, walnuts, and eggs until smooth. Heat a skillet on medium-low heat and melt lamb tallow. Make small pancakes with the batter, and carefully flip once set on one side, after 90 seconds or so.

Introduce:

- Walnuts

Detox Bath:

1 cup Seaweed Powder

Include:

o Fermented sauerkraut juice or vegetables

o Broth with every meal

o Soup at least one meal

o Cod liver oil

o Egg yolks in soup

o Crushed garlic in soup at the end

o Detox Bath

Day 13

Recipes:

- **Morning Mineral Water**
- Cod liver oil
- Avocado mashed and added to soup

Upon waking, drink 1 cup of mineral or filtered water. Allow to rest before eating.

Butternut Squash Pancakes

1 small butternut squash or other winter squash

2 cups crispy walnuts

6 eggs

1 teaspoon tallow to fry in

Peel and chop raw squash, or use cooked. In a blender, blend squash, walnuts, and eggs until smooth. Heat a skillet on medium-low heat and melt tallow. Make small pancakes with the batter, and carefully flip once set on one side, after 90 seconds or so.

Celery Root and Leek Soup

4 medium celery roots, peeled and chopped

1 bunch of celery, rinsed and sliced

4 leeks, rinsed and sliced, just the white and light green parts

4 pounds any meat; cooked chicken, chopped or beef etc.

2 quarts stock

1 tablespoon sea salt

4 cloves garlic, diced

Simmer all ingredients on low 1-2 hours or all day in the crock pot, adding garlic and cooked meat at the end 20 minutes before serving.

Stir in egg yolks. Stir in 1 teaspoon of mashed avocado.

Beef Stock:

Beef marrow bones

Filtered water

In a crockpot or stock pot, place beef marrow bones and fill to 1 inch from the top with filtered water. Simmer overnight.

Introduce:

Avocado. Be sure to puree avocado very well, using blender if desired. A little cooled stock can be added to make it into more of a 'sauce' and make it easier to puree.

Detox Bath:

1 cup Epsom salt

Include:

o Fermented sauerkraut juice or vegetables

o Broth with every meal

o Soup at least one meal

o Egg yolks in soup

o Crushed garlic in soup at the end

o Detox Bath

Day 14

Recipes:

Morning Mineral Water

Upon waking, drink 1 cup of mineral or filtered water. Allow to rest before eating.

Onion Soup

6 onions peeled and sliced thinly

2 tablespoons tallow

1 quart stock

1 quart filtered water

1 teaspoon sea salt

Directions: In a pan, melt tallow over medium low heat and add onions. Cook, covered, for 20 minutes or until onions are soft. Stir in the pan and continue cooking and stirring occasionally for 40 more minutes or until golden. Add stock, water, and tallow and simmer for an hour or all day in the crock pot.

Taco Salad Casserole

4 tomatoes

2 pounds Steak (sirloin tip is good)

2 onions

½ teaspoon sea salt

1 Anaheim chili, diced

1 cup stock

In a casserole dish, layer slices of tomatoes, cubes of steak, slices of onion. Sprinkle with chili and sea salt. Pour stock over. Cover and bake at 350* for 45 minutes. Top with

Fresh cilantro

2 cloves garlic, crushed

1 avocado, pureed

And serve.

Boiled Green Beans

1 pound green beans, simmered

2 cloves garlic, crushed

4 tablespoons tallow

Introduce:

Fresh herbs

Detox Bath:

1 cup Baking Soda

Include:

o Fermented sauerkraut juice or vegetables

o Broth with every meal

o Soup at least one meal

- Cod liver oil
- Avocado mashed and added to soup

o Egg yolks in soup

o Crushed garlic in soup at the end

o Detox Bath

Day 15

Morning Mineral Water

Upon waking, drink 1 cup of mineral or filtered water. Allow to rest before eating.

Summer Squash Intro Pancakes

1 small crookneck squash

1 cup crispy walnuts

2 eggs

1 teaspoon tallow to fry in

In a blender, blend squash, walnuts, and eggs until smooth. Heat a skillet on medium-low heat and melt lamb tallow. Make small pancakes with the batter, and carefully flip once set on one side, after 90 seconds or so.

Simmered Burgers

2 pounds ground beef

½ teaspoon sea salt

½ teaspoon pepper

2 cups stock

Mix seasonings into beef and form into patties. Simmer in stock and top with guacamole.

Guacamole:

Ingredients:

2-3 ripe avocados

2 cloves garlic

1/2 teaspoon sea salt

Directions:

Press two cloves of garlic through a garlic press. Add in 1 teaspoon of cumin, ½ a teaspoon of salt, the juice of one lemon, mix. Mash in 2-3 ripe avocados with a fork. If storing, press plastic wrap right up against the guacamole to help prevent it from oxidizing and turning brown, store in the fridge for a couple hours

Butternut Squash Soup

2 quarts stock

1 quart filtered water

4 cups pre-cut butternut squash cubes

1 tablespoon sea salt (adjust to taste)

1/2 inch ginger, peeled and grated

4 cloves garlic, crushed

Simmer all ingredients to make a soup. Puree with an immersion blender if desired for a smooth soup. Top with ginger and garlic.

Ginger Tea

1 inch ginger root, peeled and sliced into thin coins

2 quarts filtered water

* To easily peel ginger, use a spoon to rub off the skin.

Simmer ginger root in water for 10 minutes, covered. Enjoy warm or cool and enjoy cold.

Introduce:

Fresh ginger

Detox Bath:

1 cup apple cider vinegar

Include:

o Fermented sauerkraut juice or vegetables

o Broth with every meal

o Soup at least one meal

- Cod liver oil
- Avocado mashed and added to soup

o Egg yolks in soup

o Crushed garlic in soup at the end

o Detox Bath

Stage 4

Stage 4

You can eat on Stage 4:

- Meat or fish stock
- Well boiled GAPS-legal vegetables (no starchy root vegetables)
- Squash, winter and summer
- Boiled, roasted, or grilled meat (not burned)
- Sea salt
- Fresh herbs
- Cold pressed olive oil
- Fermented vegetables; saurkraut, kimchi, pickles
- Fermented fish
- Eggs
- Homemade ghee
- Stews and casseroles made with meat and vegetables
- Ripe avocado
- Pancakes made with nutbutter, squash, and eggs- fried in fat or ghee, start with one a day
- Scrambled eggs made with ghee and served with avocado if tolerated and cooked vegetables.
- Freshly pressed juices, start with a few tablespoons of carrot juice
- Bread made with nut flour, eggs, squash, tolerated fat, salt

Day 16

Recipes:

- **Morning Mineral Water**

Upon waking, drink 1 cup of mineral or filtered water. Allow to rest before eating.

Olive Oil and Fresh Herb Blend

1 quart cold pressed olive oil

1 bunch (4 ounces) basil

½ teaspoon sea salt

1-10 cloves garlic (optional)

In a blender place basil, salt, garlic, and as much olive oil as can fit. Puree until smooth. Use this 'pesto sauce' as a tasty way to get cold pressed olive oil into your meals.

*tip: a standard size (not wide mouth) quart mason jar can have a blender blade screwed on and be used as a blender container for most blenders. This saves a dish to wash!

Intro Breakfast Sausage

3 lbs ground beef

2 cloves garlic, crushed

¼ inch ginger, grated or diced

Combination of fresh basil, parsley, cilantro, or other fresh herbs, finely chopped, 2-6 tablespoons

1 teaspoons sea salt

Combine beef with seasonings, form into patties, and fry in a pan or simmer in stock until cooked through.

Summer Squash Soup

2 quarts stock

1 quart filtered water

8 small summer squash ;crookneck, zucchini, patty pan, etc

1 tablespoon sea salt (adjust to taste)

Remove stems and blossom ends from squash, coarsely chop. Simmer all ingredients to make a soup. Puree with an immersion blender if desired for a smooth soup.

Lamb Chops

8-12 lamb chops, approx. 2 inches thick

Sea salt

2 cloves garlic, crushed

Remove meat from fridge, sprinkle both sides of the chops with salt and top with crushed garlic. Allow meat to sit out, covered, for half an hour- this allows it to cook more evenly.

Move the rack in the oven to the top or second from top slot, so the meat will be about 2 inches from the element. Preheat the oven to broil on high.

Place meat on a broiler-proof pan or cookie sheet. When oven is preheated, broil for 5-7 minutes on each side, testing for doneness by cutting into the thickest lamb chop with a knife. Lamb will continue to cook a bit as it cools.

Reserve bones and drippings for stock.

Introduce:

Olive Oil

Detox Bath:

1 cup Seaweed Powder

Include:

- Cultured vegetable with every meal
- Broth with every meal
- Soup at least one meal
- Olive Oil over every meal
- Cod liver oil
- Egg yolks in soup
- Crushed garlic in soup at the end
- Avocado mashed and added to soup
- Detox Bath
- Broth with every meal

Day 17

Lamb Stock

1-2 pounds lamb marrow bones, broken to allow the marrow to come out

Filtered water

In a large stock pot, place lamb marrow bones. Fill with water to near the top and simmer for 6-8 hours or overnight in the crockpot.

Morning Mineral Water

Upon waking, drink 1 cup of mineral or filtered water. Allow to rest before eating.

Freshly Pressed Carrot Juice

Juice 1-2 carrots and try 2-3 tablespoons of carrot juice, can be mixed in with water or consumed on its own.

Butternut Squash Pancakes

1 small butternut squash

2 cups crispy walnuts

6 eggs

1 teaspoon tallow to fry in

Peel and chop raw squash, or use cooked. In a blender, blend squash, walnuts, and eggs until smooth. Heat a skillet on medium-low heat and melt tallow. Make small pancakes with the batter, and carefully flip once set on one side, after 90 seconds or so.

Chili Chicken

4 pounds chicken thighs

2 Anaheim chilies, deseeded

2 cloves garlic

1 tablespoon fresh parsley, chopped

½ teaspoon sea salt

1 quart stock

Rinse chicken and place in the bottom of a lidded casserole dish. Pour stock over the chicken, top chicken with finely diced chili, crushed garlic, parsley and sea salt. Cover and cook at 350* for 1 hour or until cooked through.

Roasted Carrot Soup

Ingredients:

5-6 large inexpensive organic juicing carrots, or more smaller ones, scrubbed.

2 large onions, peeled and quartered

6 cloves garlic, peeled

2 cups winter squash chunks, peeled and deseeded

2 tablespoons ghee or tallow

1 teaspoon unrefined sea salt

1 quart chicken stock

2 quarts filtered water

1-2 tablespoons unrefined sea salt, to taste

Directions:

Cut carrots into 3-4 inch pieces.

In an oven-safe dish (An 8x8 inch glass dish works well) pile all the vegetables, garlic, and squash. Dot across the top with ghee, and sprinkle with sea salt.

Place in the oven to roast at 300 degrees F for an hour. No need to preheat.

In a crock pot, place the roasted vegetables and drain the juices and melted ghee from the bottom of the pan into the crockpot as well. Add chicken stock and enough filtered water to cover the vegetables. Cook on low all day, or high for 4 hours.

Spoon into bowls and garnish with herbed olive oil.

Introduce:

Carrot Juice

Detox Bath:

1 cup Epsom salt

Include:

- Cultured vegetable with every meal
- Broth with every meal
- Soup at least one meal
- Olive Oil over every meal
- Cod liver oil
- Egg yolks in soup
- Crushed garlic in soup at the end
- Avocado mashed and added to soup
- Detox Bath
- Broth with every meal
- Freshly pressed juice

Day 18

Recipes:

Morning Mineral Water

Upon waking, drink 1 cup of mineral or filtered water. Allow to rest before eating.

Freshly Pressed Carrot Juice

Juice 1-2 carrots and try 2-3 tablespoons of carrot juice, can be mixed in with water or consumed on its own.

Intro Nut Flour Bread

2 cups almond flour

6 eggs

2 cups butternut squash, peeled (the neck of one medium squash)

1 teaspoon sea salt

6 tablespoons tallow to grease muffin pan

Puree all ingredients in a blender or food processor (you can keep the zucchini raw and just puree). Pour into greased muffin tins or a small loaf pan. Bake at 350* for 20 minutes, or until a knife inserted comes out clean.

Simmered Chicken and Squash

2 pounds chicken, chopped

2 pounds winter squash, peeled and chopped

1 quart stock

1 teaspoon sea salt

Simmer chicken pieces with butternut squash pieces, eat as a chunky soup.

Egg Drop Soup

6 leeks, sliced

1 quart fish stock

1 quart other stock

2 teaspoons sea salt

4 onions, sliced

4 egg yolks, beaten with a fork

Wash and slice the leeks up to where the leaves separate (use the light parts) and peel and slice the onions thinly. Simmer in stock until soft, 1 hour. Raise heat to a rapid boil and gently drip in a thin stream of egg yolks, whisking with a fork as you pour them in to make 'noodles'. Remove from heat and serve.

Introduce:

Nut flour bread

Prepare:

Soak Liver for stuffed tomatoes tomorrow.

Drain any blood from 1 pound thawed liver. Place in a bowl. Cover with the juice of one lemon and filtered water until the liver is completely covered. Cover bowl with lid or plastic wrap and return to the fridge.

Detox Bath:

1 cup Baking Soda

Include:

- Cultured vegetable with every meal
- Broth with every meal
- Soup at least one meal
- Olive Oil over every meal
- Cod liver oil
- Egg yolks in soup
- Crushed garlic in soup at the end
- Avocado mashed and added to soup
- Detox Bath
- Broth with every meal
- Freshly pressed juice

Day 19

Recipes:

Morning Mineral Water

Upon waking, drink 1 cup of mineral or filtered water. Allow to rest before eating.

Freshly Pressed Carrot Juice

Juice 1-2 carrots and try 2-3 tablespoons of carrot juice, can be mixed in with water or consumed on its own.

Scrambled Eggs with Vegetables

10 eggs, whisked

2 tablespoons tallow or ghee

¼ teaspoon sea salt

2 onions, sliced

2 avocado

In a skillet, melt tallow over medium heat. Sautee onions until soft, approx. 20 minutes. Add salt and eggs, and scramble eggs until nearly cooked through, remove before they are cooked all the way through to prevent from turning dry. Top with chunks of avocado or pureed avocado.

Stuffed Tomatoes

2 pounds ground beef

1 pound beef or chicken liver

2 cloves garlic, crushed

½ teaspoon sea salt

Fresh herbs as desired, 1 tablespoon (basil, parsley, etc)

6 large tomatoes

In a food processor, pulse to chop liver. Add to ground beef and mix in seasonings. Cut the tops off the tomatoes, and scoop out membranes and seeds using a spoon. Fill with beef mixture. Bake in a casserole dish, uncovered, for 30 minutes or until meat is cooked through. Drizzle with herbed olive oil and serve.

Veggie Stew

2 quarts chicken stock

2 pounds cubed stew meat

4 leeks, washed and sliced, just the white and light green parts

4 summer squash, chopped

2 onions, sliced

1 tablespoon sea salt (to taste)

2 carrots, cut into matchsticks

1 cup snow peas

Directions: Heat a soup pot or skillet to medium high heat, sprinkle meat with salt, then brown all sides of the meat, stirring, for about 10 minutes. Add stock, leeks, summer squash, onions, carrots, and salt and simmer for 1-2 hours. Add in snow peas 20 minutes before serving.

Soak Pecans

To soak nuts: Place 2-3 lbs raw nuts in a large bowl (they will swell, so only fill 2/3 full, using another bowl if needed). Add 2 tablespoons sea salt and cover the nuts with filtered water. Allow to soak overnight at room temperature (on the counter). No need to cover.

To dry:

Drain in a colander and start dehydrating the nuts you soaked last night, or roast in a pan as low as your oven will go. Dehydrate all day.

Chicken stock:

Ingredients

Whole chicken or chicken pieces

Directions:

Rinse chicken. Reach inside cavity and remove giblet package. Remove giblets from package and add to the stock pot. Place chicken in the stockpot.

Fill pot ¾ full with filtered water and any optional herbs and vegetables. Cook on medium-high until bubbling, then reduce heat to low and allow to simmer, covered, at least 8 hours. When done, allow to cool then pour stock through a strainer and transfer to mason jars to store in the fridge.

Do not discard the soft gelatinous parts around the bones or the skin; reserve that and use an immersion or regular blender to blend it into your stock and soups.

Pick any meat off the bones that you can after the chicken stock has been removed, reserve meat to add to soups or serve alongside. Discard the remaining bones in the pot.

Introduce:

Scrambled Eggs, liver

Detox Bath:

1 cup apple cider vinegar

Include:

- Cultured vegetable with every meal
- Broth with every meal
- Soup at least one meal
- Olive Oil over every meal
- Cod liver oil
- Egg yolks in soup
- Crushed garlic in soup at the end
- Avocado mashed and added to soup
- Detox Bath
- Broth with every meal
- Freshly pressed juice

Day 19

Day 20

- **Morning Mineral Water**

Upon waking, drink 1 cup of mineral or filtered water. Allow to rest before eating.

- **Freshly Pressed Carrot Juice**

Juice 2-3 carrots

3-4 sprigs fresh mint

Intro Breakfast Sausage

3 lbs ground beef

2 cloves garlic, crushed

¼ inch ginger, grated or diced

Combination of fresh basil, parsley, cilantro, or other fresh herbs, finely chopped, 2-6 tablespoons

1 teaspoons sea salt

Combine beef with seasonings, form into patties, and fry in a pan or simmer in stock until cooked through.

Cabbage Soup

2 head cabbage, shredded

6 carrots, shredded

1 inch ginger, grated

2 cloves garlic, crushed

1 quart stock

1 quart water

Simmer all ingredients 20 minutes, or until cabbage is soft. Top with herbed olive oil.

Sauerkraut

1 head cabbage, green or purple

2 tablespoons sea salt, course is fine

2 quart sized large mouth mason jars

Food processor or knife

Cup or cylinder that fits inside the mason jar, to smash sauerkraut

Directions:

Pack into jars, and add 1 tablespoon salt to each jar. Cover and shake to distribute the salt. Allow to sit out for an hour, until the cabbage wilts. Smash to release juices. Cover again, and allow to ferment on counter for 3 days before transferring to the fridge to store. Sauerkraut is ready to eat after the countertop fermentation.

Salmon Patties

2 pounds wild caught salmon, fresh or frozen

1 egg

½ teaspoon sea salt

Tallow or ghee to fry

In a pan with a lid, cook salmon over medium heat, turning once, until cooked through. Once salmon is cooked, allow to cool briefly (you can also just eat the salmon as is if you'd like) and then flake it with a fork, mix in the egg and salt, and form into patties. Fry over medium heat in tallow or ghee until a golden brown, approx. 5 minutes on each side.

Lamb Roast

1 boneless lamb roast

8 cloves garlic, peeled and sliced into slivers

1 tablespoon coarse salt

1 tablespoons olive oil

Remove lamb from packaging. If it is in a net, keep the netting on. If not, secure with kitchen twine by rolling the lamb into a log, and wrapping the twine around the roast every 1-2 inches and tying. Place the lamb on a baking dish and preheat oven to 400*. Using a paring or steak knife, make slits every 3-4 inches across the top of the lamb in a loose grid about 1 inch deep. Insert a sliver of garlic into each slice, pushing the garlic as far in as you can (this is illustrated on the website). Sprinkle the roast with coarse salt and drizzle with olive oil. Bake until an internal temperature reaches 140*, checking at 45 minutes and periodically thereafter. Remove from oven and allow to rest for at least 30 minutes, lamb will continue to rise in temperature as it rests. After resting, remove netting or twine and slice to serve.

Introduce: Additions to fresh juice

Detox Bath: 1 cup Seaweed Powder

Include:

- Cultured vegetable with every meal
- Broth with every meal
- Soup at least one meal
- Olive Oil over every meal
- Cod liver oil
- Egg yolks in soup
- Crushed garlic in soup at the end
- Avocado mashed and added to soup
- Detox Bath
- Broth with every meal
- Freshly pressed juice

Stage 5

You can eat on Stage 5:

- Meat or fish stock
- Raw legal vegetables, peeled
- Squash, winter and summer
- Peeled, cooked apple, pureed
- Honey, up to a couple tablespoons a day
- Boiled, roasted, or grilled meat (not burned)
- Sea salt
- Fresh herbs
- Cold pressed olive oil
- Fermented vegetables; sauerkraut, kimchi, pickles, etc
- Fermented fish
- Eggs
- Homemade ghee
- Stews and casseroles made with meat and vegetables
- Ripe avocado mashed into soups, starting with 1-3 teaspoons a day
- Pancakes made with nutbutter, squash, and eggs- fried in fat or ghee
- Freshly pressed juices, carrot, mint, cabbage, lettuce, apple, pineapple, mango
- Bread made with nut flour, eggs, squash, tolerated fat, salt

Day 21

Recipes:

Freshly Pressed Carrot Juice

Juice:

3 carrots

4 sprigs of mint

Raw Intro Salad

1 English cucumber, peeled and sliced.

1 head soft butter lettuce, rinsed and torn

Herbed olive oil

Toss salad with herbed olive oil, sprinkle with salt if desired.

Cauliflower Soup

2 pounds cauliflower

1 quart stock

1 quart water

2 cloves garlic, crushed

1 teaspoon sea salt (to taste)

Simmer all ingredients, puree until smooth.

Drumsticks

8 Chicken drumsticks

6 summer squash

4 onions, peeled and quartered

Sea salt to taste

Bake drumsticks (or roast a whole chicken) surrounded by chopped squash and onions for 30 minutes, or until cooked through. Reserve bones for stock.

Roast Vegetables

1 pound cauliflower florets

3 large carrots

1 celery root, peeled and chopped (optional)

3 stalks of celery, chopped

1 pound asparagus, chopped (if in season)

¼ cup olive oil

½ teaspoon sea salt

2 tablespoons dried basil or other seasoning blend

Toss veggies with sea salt, olive oil, and seasoning. Place into a 9x13 " glass oven safe dish. Cook at 400 Degrees for 45 minutes

Make Chicken stock

Stock and Onion Gravy

By now you may be getting tired of the broth with every meal. This stock and onion gravy is a great way to sneak it in! Like the herbed olive oil, it's easy to spoon over meats and vegetables.

1 pot chicken stock

6 onions, peeled and sliced

1 teaspoon sea salt

Simmer onions in chicken stock, covered, until onions are soft. Add 1 teaspoon sea salt and puree with an immersion blender. Remove lid and reduce over low heat until desired consistency (reduced by half is good). Store in glass jars in the fridge and spoon over meats, add to scrambled eggs, and use to sauté veggies in.

Introduce:

Raw Cucumber and soft lettuce

Detox Bath:

1 cup Epsom salt

Include:

- Cultured vegetable with every meal
- Broth with every meal
- Soup at least one meal
- Olive Oil over every meal
- Cod liver oil
- Egg yolks in soup
- Crushed garlic in soup at the end
- Avocado mashed and added to soup
- Detox Bath
- Broth with every meal
- Freshly pressed juice

Day 22

Recipes:

Morning Mineral Water

Upon waking, drink 1 cup of mineral or filtered water. Allow to rest before eating.

Freshly Pressed Carrot Juice

Juice:

3 carrots

4 sprigs of mint

Summer Squash Intro Pancakes

1 small crookneck squash

1 cup crispy walnuts

2 eggs

1 teaspoon lamb tallow to fry in

In a blender, blend squash, walnuts, and eggs until smooth. Heat a skillet on medium-low heat and melt lamb tallow. Make small pancakes with the batter, and carefully flip once set on one side, after 90 seconds or so.

Butter Lettuce Salad

1 head butter lettuce, torn

1 tomato, cubed

1 onion, diced

Mix salad and top with bacon if desired and dressing below.

Grilled Crispy Bacon

1 pound bacon, sugar and nitrate free (we use beef bacon from US Wellness)

On a large griddle over two burners, or in two skillets, fry bacon over medium heat. Turn once the edges start to brown. Once cooked, remove to paper towels to drain, serve warm.

Reserve bacon drippings in the fridge to use for cooking later on- bacon drippings add a fantastic flavor to just about anything!

Basil Garlic Dressing

This is similar to the herbed olive oil and can be poured over foods as well

4 ounces fresh basil

3 cups cold pressed olive oil

6 cloves garlic

Puree all ingredients, using a quart small mouth mason jar fitted with the blender blade if desired. Pour over salads and meats.

Meatballs

These meatballs are packed with veggies for flavor, moisture, and nutrition

3 pounds ground beef (or other ground meat)

1 carrot

1 onion

1 zucchini

1 teaspoon sea salt

½ teaspoon freshly ground black pepper

¼ cup onion gravy from yesterday

Using a food processor or grater, grate the carrot, onion, and zucchini. Mix in with the meat, adding in salt and pepper. Form into balls. Pour gravy over meatballs and then bake at 375* for 30 minutes, or until cooked through.

Summer Squash Soup

2 quarts stock

1 quart filtered water

8 small summer squash ;crookneck, zucchini, patty pan, etc

1 tablespoon sea salt (adjust to taste)

Remove stems and blossom ends from squash, coarsely chop. Simmer all ingredients to make a soup. Puree with an immersion blender if desired for a smooth soup.

Introduce:

Tomatoes, carrots, onion

Detox Bath:

1 cup Baking Soda

Include:

- Cultured vegetable with every meal
- Broth with every meal
- Soup at least one meal
- Olive Oil over every meal
- Cod liver oil
- Egg yolks in soup
- Crushed garlic in soup at the end
- Avocado mashed and added to soup
- Detox Bath
- Broth with every meal
- Freshly pressed juice

Day 23

Recipes:

- **Morning Mineral Water**
- **Freshly Pressed Carrot Juice**

Upon waking, drink 1 cup of mineral or filtered water. Allow to rest before eating.

Juice:

3 carrots

4 sprigs of mint

Scrambled Eggs with Vegetables

10 eggs, whisked

2 tablespoons tallow or ghee

¼ teaspoon sea salt

2 onions, sliced

2 avocado

In a skillet, melt tallow over medium heat. Sautee onions until soft, approx. 20 minutes. Add salt and eggs, and scramble eggs until nearly cooked through, remove before they are cooked all the way through to prevent from turning dry. Top with chunks of avocado or pureed avocado.

Creamy Cauliflower

2 pounds cauliflower

1 quart stock

½ teaspoon salt

4 tablespoons lamb tallow

Boil cauliflower until soft, 20 minutes. Drain, reserving stock for use in soup. "Butter" the cauliflower with tallow and sprinkle with salt.

Baked Salmon

This baked salmon is slow-baked right on the serving platter- no mess, no fuss!

2 wild-caught salmon filets - about a pound each

2 Tablespoons Dill

2 Tablespoons Thyme

1/2 teaspoon pepper

1/2 teasoon sea salt

1 teaspoon olive oil

Directions:

Heat the oven to 200 F. (not a typo)

Mix dill, thyme, pepper, and sea salt.

Grease an oven proof serving platter with olive oil. Place salmon filets on there, and drizzel with olive oil. Sprinkle with herbs.

Bake for about 40 to 45 minutes, until salmon flakes.

Tomato slices with Basil

Slice 4 tomatoes, sprinkle with chopped fresh basil and sprinkle with ½ teaspoon sea salt.

Celery Root and Leek Soup

4 medium celery roots, peeled and chopped

1 bunch of celery, rinsed and sliced

4 leeks, rinsed and sliced, just the white and light green parts

4 pounds any meat; cooked chicken, chopped or beef etc.

2 quarts stock

1 tablespoon sea salt

4 cloves garlic, diced

Simmer all ingredients on low 1-2 hours or all day in the crock pot, adding garlic and cooked meat at the end 20 minutes before serving.

Fish Stock

2 pounds fish with bones and scales.

Filtered water

Directions: Simmer whole fish in water for 8 hours. Strain meat and bones. Set meat aside to add to soup, store broth as needed in mason jars.

Introduce:

Raw Cabbage

Detox Bath:

1 cup apple cider vinegar

Include:

- Cultured vegetable with every meal
- Broth with every meal
- Soup at least one meal
- Olive Oil over every meal
- Cod liver oil
- Egg yolks in soup
- Crushed garlic in soup at the end
- Avocado mashed and added to soup
- Detox Bath
- Broth with every meal
- Freshly pressed juice

Day 24

Recipes:

Freshly Pressed Juice

Juice:

6 carrots

2 cucumbers

4 sprigs of mint

Apple Sauce

6 ripe apples

½ cup filtered water

Peel and core apples. Thinly slice and simmer in a saucepan with the water, covered, until very soft. Mash with a fork and eat with ghee or tallow.

Butternut Squash Pancakes

1 small butternut squash

2 cups crispy walnuts

6 eggs

1 teaspoon tallow to fry in

Peel and chop raw squash, or use cooked. In a blender, blend squash, walnuts, and eggs until smooth. Heat a skillet on medium-low heat and melt tallow. Make small pancakes with the batter, and carefully flip once set on one side, after 90 seconds or so.

Beef Roast in the Crockpot

1 beef roast, 3-6 lbs

1 pound pearl onions, peeled

4 carrots, cut into chunks

6 summer squash, cut into chunks

4 cloves garlic, crushed

1 sprig fresh rosemary

1 tablespoon sea salt

In a crock pot, place beef roast. Cover with garlic and rosemary. Place vegetables around beef, and sprinkle everything with sea salt. Cook on low all day or high for 4 hours. Spoon drippings over beef to serve.

Onion Soup

6 onions peeled and sliced thinly

2 tablespoons tallow

1 quart stock

1 quart filtered water

1 teaspoon sea salt

Directions: In a pan, melt tallow over medium low heat and add onions. Cook, covered, for 20 minutes or until onions are soft. Stir in the pan and continue cooking and stirring occasionally for 40 more minutes or until golden. Add stock, water, and tallow and simmer for an hour or all day in the crock pot.

Beef Stock:

Beef marrow bones

Filtered water

In a crockpot or stock pot, place beef marrow bones and fill to 1 inch from the top with filtered water. Simmer overnight.

> *Many people have trouble with fruits, so watch for reactions in digestion, attention, bed wetting, behavior, and any other common symptom that you or your family members experience. Hopefully after getting this far through the intro you will tolerate this well!*

Introduce:

Apple sauce

Detox Bath:

1 cup Seaweed Powder

Include:

- Cultured vegetable with every meal
- Broth with every meal
- Soup at least one meal
- Olive Oil over every meal
- Cod liver oil
- Egg yolks in soup
- Crushed garlic in soup at the end
- Avocado mashed and added to soup
- Detox Bath
- Broth with every meal
- Freshly pressed juice

Day 25

Recipes:

Morning Mineral Water

Upon waking, drink 1 cup of mineral or filtered water. Allow to rest before eating.

Freshly Pressed Juice

Juice:

6 carrots

2 cucumbers

½ red beet

4 sprigs of mint

Egg and Squash Bake

6 eggs

1 neck of a medium butternut squash

1 teaspoon sea salt

1 tablespoon tallow

Peel squash and cut into chunks. Puree or grate in food processor. Add in eggs and sea salt. Grease 8x8 glass dish with tallow and pour in egg mixture. Bake at 350* for 20 minutes, or until set in the center.

Chicken Liver Pate

1 pound of chicken livers, washed

2 medium white or yellow onions, minced

3 cloves garlic, minced

1 teaspoon thyme

1/4 cup tallow + 2 tablespoons

1 two-ounce can of anchovies

Instructions

Over high heat in a large saucepan, heat tallow until melted then add onions, stir, cooking for about 5 minutes, or until softened, add garlic and thyme, cook for a minute or two more. Remove from heat, drain excess liquid, and pour this into food processor.

Using the remaining two tablespoons of butter, melt over medium heat. Add liver and cook until the outside is done, but the inside is still pink. Drain.

To food processor add:

1 two-ounce can of anchovies

Process until well pureed and all of the ingredients are well combined.

Form pates by lining 3 custard dishes or small ramekins with plastic wrap. Spread in pate, and place two in the freezer for later, one in the fridge. Turn out, and remove plastic wrap to serve. Stir into soups, or use on top of nut flour bread.

Intro Broccoli Beef Soup

3 pounds hamburger

2 pounds broccoli

2 pounds cauliflower

2 quarts stock

1 tablespoon sea salt

Simmer all ingredients, breaking up hamburger as it cooks.

Introduce:

Raw honey- spread some raw honey on a piece of nutflour bread or pancakes.

Detox Bath:

1 cup Epsom salt

Include:

- Fermented vegetables
- Broth with every meal
- Soup at least one meal
- Egg yolks in soup
- Crushed garlic in soup right before eating
- Cod Liver Oil
- Olive Oil
- Freshly Pressed Juice
- Detox Bath

Stage 6

Stage 6

You can eat on Stage 6:

- Meat or fish stock
- Raw legal vegetables, peeled
- Squash, winter and summer
- Peeled, raw apple
- Other fruits, raw, introduce slowly
- Honey, up to a couple tablespoons a day
- Boiled, roasted, or grilled meat (not burned)
- Sea salt
- Fresh herbs
- Cold pressed olive oil
- Fermented vegetables; sauerkraut, kimchi, pickles, etc.
- Fermented fish
- Egg yolk, organic, carefully separated from the white
- Homemade ghee
- Stews and casseroles made with meat and vegetables
- Ripe avocado mashed into soups
- Pancakes made with nutbutter, squash, and eggs- fried in fat or
- Scrambled eggs made with ghee and served with avocado if tolerated and cooked vegetables.
- Freshly pressed juices, carrot, mint, cabbage, lettuce, apple, pineapple, mango
- Bread made with nut flour, eggs, squash, tolerated fat, salt- use dates and dried fruit to sweeten.

Day 26

Recipes:

Morning Mineral Water

Upon waking, drink 1 cup of mineral or filtered water. Allow to rest before eating.

Freshly Pressed Juice

Juice:

6 carrots

2 cucumbers

½ beet

4 sprigs of mint

Scrambled Eggs with Vegetables

10 eggs, whisked

2 tablespoons tallow or ghee

¼ teaspoon sea salt

2 onions, sliced

2 avocado

In a skillet, melt tallow over medium heat. Sautee onions until soft, approx. 20 minutes. Add salt and eggs, and scramble eggs until nearly cooked through, remove before they are cooked all the way through to prevent from turning dry. Top with chunks of avocado or pureed avocado.

Raw Apple and Cabbage Salad

1 apple, peeled and shredded

¼ cabbage head, shredded

½ teaspoon fresh ginger, peeled and diced

Toss ingredients together.

Make Chicken stock

Intro Breakfast Sausage

3 lbs ground beef

2 cloves garlic, crushed

¼ inch ginger, grated or diced

Combination of fresh basil, parsley, cilantro, or other fresh herbs, finely chopped, 2-6 tablespoons

1 teaspoons sea salt

Combine beef with seasonings, form into patties, and fry in a pan or simmer in stock until cooked through.

Cauliflower Soup

2 pounds cauliflower

1 quart stock

1 quart water

2 cloves garlic, crushed

1 teaspoon sea salt (to taste)

Simmer all ingredients, puree until smooth.

Introduce:

Raw Apple, peeled and cored

Detox Bath:

1 cup Baking Soda

Include:

o Fermented vegetables

o Broth with every meal

o Soup at least one meal

o Egg yolks in soup

o Crushed garlic in soup right before eating

o Cod Liver Oil

o Olive Oil

o Freshly Pressed Juice

o Detox Bath

Day 27

Recipes:

- **Morning Mineral Water**

Upon waking, drink 1 cup of mineral or filtered water. Allow to rest before eating.

Freshly Pressed Juice

Juice:

¼ head cabbage

4 carrots

½ beet

1 green apple

Summer Squash Intro Pancakes

1 small crookneck squash

1 cup crispy walnuts

2 eggs

1 teaspoon lamb tallow to fry in

In a blender, blend squash, walnuts, and eggs until smooth. Heat a skillet on medium-low heat and melt lamb tallow. Make small pancakes with the batter, and carefully flip once set on one side, after 90 seconds or so.

Butternut Squash and Beef Casserole

2 pounds hamburger

1 large butternut squash (3 pounds)

½ teaspoon sea salt

2 cups stock

Tallow or fat to grease pan

Preheat oven to 350* Mix hamburger with sea salt. Peel and remove pulp from butternut squash, and chop into bite-sized pieces. Grease a 9x13" pan with fat. Place squash in the pan and pour stock over the squash. Place pieces of the raw hamburger over the top of the squash, covering evenly. Bake uncovered for 45 minutes or until squash is soft and beef is cooked.

Chicken Curry Soup

2 tablespoons tallow or ghee

1 Anaheim chili

4 onions, sliced

½ inch ginger root, peeled and grated

1 quart stock

1 quart filtered water

4 cups cooked chicken, diced

6 cloves garlic, crushed

In the bottom of a pot, sauté onions, ginger, and pepper in tallow until onions are soft. Add stock and water and bring to a simmer. Add chicken and cook 20 minutes, or until heated through. Top with garlic and serve.

Beef Stock:

Beef marrow bones

Filtered water

In a crockpot or stock pot, place beef marrow bones and fill to 1 inch from the top with filtered water. Simmer overnight.

Introduce:

Raw sliced pears

Detox Bath:

1 cup apple cider vinegar

Include:

o Fermented vegetables

o Broth with every meal

o Soup at least one meal

o Egg yolks in soup

o Crushed garlic in soup right before eating

o Cod Liver Oil

o Olive Oil

o Freshly Pressed Juice

o Detox Bath

Day 28

Recipes:

Morning Mineral Water

Upon waking, drink 1 cup of mineral or filtered water. Allow to rest before eating.

Freshly Pressed Juice

Juice:

1 bunch celery

1 bunch parsley

2 carrots

2 green apples

Fruit Salad

4 apples

4 pears

4 ripe bananas

Meatball-vegetable soup:

Ingredients:

1 quart chicken stock,

4 teaspoons sea salt,

1 quart filtered water,

8-10 meatballs,

4 cups of chopped vegetables (brocccoli, carrots, onions, spinach, tomatoes, squash; whatever combination you'd like).

Directions:

Add stock, water, salt, tomato paste, vegetables to crock pot and cook on low all day. Add meatballs during the last 30 minutes of cooking to heat thoroughly. When serving, evenly distribute meatballs among bowls with the soup.

Meatballs:

3 lbs of ground beef

1 teaspoon sea salt

1 tablespoon basil, diced

1 clove garlic, crushed

Fry in:

2 tablespoons beef tallow or coconut oil

Mix everything with a fork, or by hand. Shape into walnut sized balls and fry in a skillet with the fat over medium heat, gently turning the meatballs during cooking to make sure all sides get cooked. Fry until browned on the outside, cutting one open to make sure they are no longer pink on the inside.

Introduce:

Bananas. Bananas covered in brown spots are allowed on the GAPS diet. Avoid any bananas that still have green on them, they are too starchy.

Detox Bath:

1 cup Seaweed Powder

Include:

- Cultured vegetable with every meal
- Broth with every meal
- Soup at least one meal
- Olive Oil over every meal
- Cod liver oil
- Egg yolks in soup
- Crushed garlic in soup at the end
- Avocado mashed and added to soup
- Detox Bath
- Broth with every meal
- Freshly pressed juice

Day 29

Recipes:

Morning Mineral Water

Upon waking, drink 1 cup of mineral or filtered water. Allow to rest before eating.

Freshly Pressed Juice

Juice:

6 carrots

2 cucumbers

4 sprigs of mint

Apple Chutney

Apples, peeled and chopped; to fill a quart jar (6 or so)

Juice of 2 lemons

2 tablespoons honey

1/2 cup raisins

2 inches of hot chili pepper, fresh and de-seeded

1 teaspoon fennel seeds

Mix all ingredients, place in jar. Pack gently to start to release the juices. If needed, add filtered water to cover the fruit. Cover and leave at room temperature for 2 days, transferring to the refrigerator for up to 2 months.

Discard the chili pepper after the 2-day fermentation at room temperature.

Baked Honey Mustard Chicken

3 pounds boneless chicken thighs

¼ cup prepared mustard, natural

2 tablespoons honey

2 tablespoons tallow

Grease a 9x13 glass casserole with tallow. Preheat oven to 375*. Mix mustard and honey in a shallow dish and coat chicken with it. Place chicken in casserole dish, skin side up if there is skin, and bake for 35 minutes or until juices run clear.

Fish Stock

2 pounds fish with bones and scales.

Filtered water

Directions: Simmer whole fish in water for 8 hours. Strain meat and bones. Set meat aside to add to soup, store broth as needed in mason jars.

Smooth Carrot Soup with Squash and Garlic

5-10 large carrots, scrubbed

6 small to medium summer squash

4 cloves garlic, peeled and minced

2 quarts stock

1 tablespoon sea salt (to taste)

Filtered water

Chop carrots and squash and place in pot. Add stock, salt, and then add water to fill pot or crock pot. Simmer 2 hours on the stove or cook all day in the crockpot. Add garlic just before serving. Puree with immersion blender and add in meat chunks if desired after pureeing.

'Meal' Salad

Meal salads are wonderful for spring and summer. Crunchy greens with lots of toppings.

1 pound greens; spinach, lettuce, cabbage

2 tomatoes, chopped

1 onion, diced

1 cup crispy nuts, chopped

½ cup sunflower seeds

1 pound chicken, cooked, sliced

Layer all ingredients and toss with dressing right before serving. Top with herbed olive oil.

Detox Bath:

1 cup Epsom salt

Include:

- Cultured vegetable with every meal
- Broth with every meal
- Soup at least one meal
- Olive Oil over every meal
- Cod liver oil
- Egg yolks in soup
- Crushed garlic in soup at the end
- Avocado mashed and added to soup
- Detox Bath
- Broth with every meal
- Freshly pressed juice

Day 30

Recipes:

- **Morning Mineral Water**
- **Freshly Pressed Juice**

Upon waking, drink 1 cup of mineral or filtered water. Allow to rest before eating.

Juice:

1 bunch celery

1 bunch parsley

2 carrots

2 green apples

Zucchini Bread

2 cups almond flour

6 eggs

2-3 medium zucchini

½ teaspoon sea salt

2 tablespoons tallow

Puree all ingredients in a blender or food processor (you can keep the zucchini raw and just puree). Pour into greased muffin tins or a small loaf pan. Bake at 350* for 30-45 minutes, or until a knife inserted comes out clean.

Lamb Roast

1 boneless lamb roast

8 cloves garlic, peeled and sliced into slivers

1 tablespoon coarse salt

1 tablespoons olive oil

Remove lamb from packaging. If it is in a net, keep the netting on. If not, secure with kitchen twine by rolling the lamb into a log, and wrapping the twine around the roast every 1-2 inches and tying. Place the lamb on a baking dish and preheat oven to 400*. Using a paring or steak knife, make slits every 3-4 inches across the top of the lamb in a loose grid about 1 inch deep. Insert a sliver of garlic into each slice, pushing the garlic as far in as you can (this is illustrated on the website). Sprinkle the roast with coarse salt and drizzle with olive oil. Bake until an internal temperature reaches 140*, checking at 45 minutes and periodically thereafter. Remove from oven and allow to rest for at least 30 minutes, lamb will continue to rise in temperature as it rests. After resting, remove netting or twine and slice to serve.

Roast Vegetables

1 pound cauliflower florets

3 large carrots

1 celery root, peeled and chopped (optional)

3 stalks of celery, chopped

¼ cup tallow

½ teaspoon sea salt

2 tablespoons dried basil or other seasoning blend

Toss veggies with sea salt, olive oil, and seasoning. Place into a 9x13 " glass oven safe dish. Cook at 400 Degrees for 45 minutes

Detox Bath:

1 cup Baking Soda

Include:

- Cultured vegetable with every meal
- Broth with every meal
- Soup at least one meal
- Olive Oil over every meal
- Cod liver oil
- Egg yolks in soup
- Crushed garlic in soup at the end
- Avocado mashed and added to soup
- Detox Bath
- Broth with every meal
- Freshly pressed juice

Introducing Dairy

Introducing Dairy

Dairy can be introduced during the introduction diet, or not. I left the directions out because so many people need to really heal their gut lining before attempting dairy.

The reading about dairy starts on page 119 in the GAPS book.

Introduce dairy products in this order, doing a sensitivity test of placing a drop of the potential food on the wrist of your GAPS patient before bed, allowing it to dry, and then seeing if a reaction occurred overnight.

- Ghee, on the second phase of the intro diet
- Butter, organic and unsalted, after 6 weeks on the diet
- Whey
  - Sensitivity test
  - 1 teaspoon/day of whey added to meat stock or soup
  - After 1-5 days, increase to 2 teaspoons of whey/day
  - Increase whey in this manner until ½ to 1 cup of whey is consumed
- Sour Cream (cultured cream using a yogurt culture)
- Yogurt made with full fat milk
- Kefir and sour cream made with kefir culture
  - Asiago
  - Brie
  - Camembert
  - Cheddar
  - Colby
  - Gorgonzola
  - Gouda
  - Havarti

- Monterey Jack
- Muenster
- Parmesan
- Roquefort
- Romano
- Stilton
- Swiss
- Uncreamed cottage cheese (dry curd)

Dairy Recipes

24-hour SCD Yogurt

Commercial yogurt is not allowed as it has not been incubated long enough to use up all the lactose. The 24-hour incubation at 100 degrees F gives the culture sufficient time to use up the vast majority of the lactose, making yogurt acceptable on the diet.

Ingredients:

½ gallon milk for yogurt or cream for cultured cream (goat or cow, raw or pasteurized. Preferably raw and from cows or goats eating fresh pasture)

Yogurt starter, plain high quality yogurt from the health food store can be used as the starter.

Directions:

In a stock pot, heat milk gently on medium heat, stirring approximately every 10 minutes, until milk is close to a boil.

Cover, remove from burner, and allow to cool until the yogurt is comfortable to the touch, 90-110* F.

Make sure the yogurt is not too hot at this stage, or you will kill the good bacteria that are going to make your yogurt into milk.

Pour nearly warm milk into jars, I use quart sized jars usually.

Using one tablespoon of commercial yogurt per quart, mix yogurt starter into the jars of warm milk.

Cover, and shake to distribute culture.

Keep warm in a yogurt maker, Excalibur dehydrator, or cooler at 100 degrees for a full 24 hours. Yogurt is now done and should be kept in the refrigerator.

Drip Yogurt to make yogurt cheese and whey

Ingredients:

2 cups yogurt

Equipment:

1 coffee filter, double layer of cheese cloth, or thin very clean dish towel

Sieve

Bowl that the sieve can easily rest over without touching the bottom.

Directions: Put the sieve into the bowl, then the coffee filter, clean cloth, or cheesecloth in the sieve. Pour in 2 cups of yogurt. Cover with plastic wrap and place in the fridge all day or overnight. What remains is yogurt cheese, transfer cheese to a sealed container and use within a couple days or freeze for later use.

What dripped out is whey, reserve this in a mason jar with a lid for a month or two.

After Intro

After the GAPS Intro

Coconut on Intro: Fats on the Introduction Diet should come from animal products- at first tallow and chicken fat is allowed, later on ghee (clarified butter) as tolerated

I hope by now you are feeling so much better!
Introducing more foods

After the GAPS introduction diet you can slowly add in the rest of the GAPS legal foods: Cultured dairy (if you haven't already), coconut products, soaked beans, sprouted beans, more whole crispy nuts, seeds, dried fruit, and meat jerky.

Supplements you may find helpful

You may also wish to add in supplements that you think were helping you before going off them for the intro, being careful to introduce them one at a time and note any side effects to evaluate if they are something helpful or not.

Using the Regular Grain Free Meal Plan

If you have found this 30-day guide helpful, you also will find the Grain Free Meal Plan helpful- I plan out shopping lists, meals, and snacks for you so that you don't have to come up with dinner every night. It's also easy to just cross out and insert other meals if you want to substitute your family's favorites.

Made in the USA
Charleston, SC
17 February 2017